Original title:
Good Habits Now

Author: Clement Portlander
ISBN HARDBACK: 978-9916-88-280-1
ISBN PAPERBACK: 978-9916-88-281-8

Gentle Reminders of Progress

Each step we take is a seed we sow,
In quiet moments, our spirits grow.
With every doubt that we leave behind,
A brighter path we slowly find.

The light within us starts to gleam,
Shining brightly, a hopeful dream.
Let's cherish each small win we make,
And let the past not hold us awake.

Anchors in the Storm

When thunder roars and shadows fall,
We seek the steadiness through it all.
With friends beside us, hearts entwined,
We weather the storm, our strength defined.

In darkness deep, we'll find our way,
Guided by love, come what may.
These anchors hold, keep us secure,
In every tempest, we will endure.

The Journey of One Thousand Choices

With every breath, a chance to take,
Paths unfold with each decision we make.
Some may lead to joy and light,
Others to lessons, but all feel right.

We gather moments, a tapestry spun,
Through winding roads, and under the sun.
The choices linger, shaping our core,
Navigating life, we always explore.

Rituals of Resilience

In morning light, we rise anew,
A cup of tea, a quiet view.
With grounding breaths, we face the day,
Embracing challenges that come our way.

Through every trial, we learn to bend,
With open hearts, we will transcend.
For in the struggle, strength is found,
In rituals sacred, we're safe and sound.

Cultivating Tomorrow's Seeds

In the earth we plant our dreams,
Nurturing hope with tender seams.
Each seed a whisper, each sprout a song,
Together they grow, where hearts belong.

Sunlight dances on emerald leaves,
A promise kept, as nature weaves.
With patient hands, we tend the ground,
In silent joy, our roots are found.

Gentle Daily Rituals

Morning light spills through the trees,
A soft embrace in the gentle breeze.
Moments cherished in mindful grace,
Each breath a step to a sacred place.

With steaming tea and whispered thoughts,
In stillness, we connect the dots.
These daily acts, a loving embrace,
Ground us in time, a measured pace.

Steps to the Sunrise

With each dawn, a path unfolds,
Golden light in stories told.
Footprints leading past the night,
Steps to greet the morning light.

A tapestry of colors bright,
Whispers of hope in the soft twilight.
Together we rise, hand in hand,
United in dreams that brightly stand.

Embracing the Unseen

Beneath the surface, life does stir,
In quiet corners, dreams confer.
The pulse of hope beats deep within,
A dance of shadows where we begin.

Silence holds a myriad of tales,
In unseen depths, our spirit sails.
Weaving light with threads of night,
In unity, we find our sight.

Blossoms of Intent

In the garden of dreams we sow,
Seeds of hope begin to grow.
Whispers of love in gentle winds,
Nurtured by faith, the journey begins.

Colors bloom beneath the sun,
Every petal is a story spun.
With every sunrise, brighter days,
In this dance, our hearts ablaze.

Embracing the Power of Perseverance

Through the storms and darkest nights,
We rise up, igniting lights.
With each challenge, strength we find,
A relentless spirit, unconfined.

Brick by brick, we build our way,
With courage that guides us every day.
In the face of doubt, we stand tall,
Falling down, but rising after all.

The Echo of Daily Intentions

Upon the dawn, intentions clear,
A vow to shine, to persevere.
In simple moments, we will find,
The echoes of a focused mind.

Each breath a promise, softly spoken,
In every heart, no dream is broken.
From morning's light to evening's glow,
Our daily paths will surely show.

Masterpieces in the Making

Each stroke of life, a canvas wide,
In colors bold, and hopes untried.
Brush in hand, we paint our way,
Creating dreams from night to day.

Every challenge, a hue refined,
Patience the key, with love aligned.
In this gallery, hearts will sing,
Masterpieces, to life we bring.

Seeds of Yesterday

In the soil of time we plant,
Dreams that sway like gentle chant.
Whispers of hopes buried deep,
Stories of love our hearts keep.

Memories dance in twilight glow,
Tracing the paths where we dared go.
Roots entwined in timeless grace,
Nurturing youth to embrace.

Harvest of Today

Golden fields under bright sun,
Each moment a race begun.
Hands that toil with heart and might,
Gather joy from morning light.

Crops of laughter, fields of cheer,
Bountiful gifts, year after year.
Together we reap what we sow,
As the winds of fortune blow.

Crafting a Life of Purpose

With every choice, we shape our route,
Chasing dreams, there's no doubt.
Molding clay of hopes and fears,
Building strength through all the years.

Each step taken with intent,
Finding joy in time well spent.
Weaving stories, hearts align,
A tapestry of stars that shine.

Harmony in the Mundane

In the rhythm of daily grind,
Simple joys are intertwined.
Finding peace in moments small,
Listening to the life's soft call.

A cup of tea, the morning light,
Laughter shared, a warm invite.
Every tick of the clock, divine,
In the ordinary, we find shine.

Unseen Foundations of Growth

Beneath the surface, roots extend,
Silent strength that does not bend.
In the dark, the whispers grow,
Fueling life with gentle flow.

Time nurtures what we can't see,
Hope unfurls with mystery.
From humble seeds, greatness flows,
In unseen paths, potential glows.

Cultivating Tomorrow's Success

In fields of dreams we sow the seeds,
With care and hope, we meet our needs.
Each choice we make, a path to clear,
Towards a future we hold dear.

With patience strong, we tend the growth,
Nurturing visions, embracing both.
The journey starts with every stride,
Tomorrow's light, a hopeful guide.

Through storms and sun, we learn to stand,
United, driven, heart in hand.
As nature bends but won't forget,
The strength within, our surest bet.

So let us rise, with purpose bold,
In each small step, success unfolds.
Together we'll shape what's meant to be,
Cultivating futures, wild and free.

The Art of Daily Discoveries

Each morning brings a brand-new light,
A canvas fresh, a chance to write.
With curious hearts, we seek to find,
The hidden gems that spark the mind.

In simple things, we find our muse,
A whisper, glimmer, subtle clues.
The rustling leaves, the call of birds,
In nature's chatter, sweetest words.

Through every glance, a story waits,
In vibrant colors, joyful fates.
With every step, we take the chance,
To dance with life, a sweet romance.

Let's cherish these small revelations,
Embrace the art of inspirations.
For in the everyday we see,
The magic of what life can be.

Small Steps Toward Greatness

With every morning, we awake,
To dreams unleashed, new paths we'll take.
A step so small, yet full of grace,
The journey starts in this sacred space.

Each action counts, each choice we make,
A ripple starts, a wave to break.
In perseverance, strength is found,
Small steps lead to solid ground.

With courage held, we push on through,
Believing big, in all we do.
In every stumble, lessons grow,
Our spirit shines, our hearts aglow.

So take that leap, let courage reign,
In each small win, we feel no pain.
Together, moving toward the light,
Small steps toward a future bright.

Embrace the Everyday

In daily moments, life unfolds,
In laughter shared, in hands we hold.
The quiet nights and bustling days,
A tapestry of countless ways.

Through mundane tasks, we play our part,
In every beat, we share our heart.
With open eyes, we seek the grace,
In simple joys, we find our place.

Let's treasure each breath, each sigh,
In fleeting seconds, time slips by.
With gratitude, we'll ease our fears,
And celebrate the passing years.

So take a moment, pause and feel,
The beauty in what's truly real.
In every heartbeat, find the way,
To embrace the gift of every day.

A Tapestry of Intentions

Threads of dreams entwined in one,
Weaving hopes beneath the sun.
Each intention, a vibrant hue,
Crafting visions, bright and true.

Gentle whispers, guiding hands,
Mapping futures where love stands.
Each stitch a promise, firm and fast,
A legacy, forever cast.

In the loom of life we shared,
Every moment, cherished, cared.
Together we will write our fate,
A tapestry that will not wait.

As we navigate the night,
With our hearts as guiding light.
Intentions strong, we'll not forget,
In this fabric we beget.

Foundations Built with Care

In the soil, deep roots are sown,
A silent strength, yet brightly grown.
Brick by brick, we build our home,
In whispered dreams, we kindly roam.

Patience molds each sturdy wall,
Bearing witness to our call.
Caring hands lay every stone,
In this sanctuary, we find our own.

With every layer, trust takes flight,
Anchored hearts, a timeless sight.
Foundations strong, our lives entwine,
In love's embrace, we brightly shine.

When storms rage and shadows loom,
With care, we'll banish every gloom.
Together, as we rise and dare,
Our spirits soar, foundations rare.

Pathways of Purpose

Winding trails beneath the trees,
Whispers carried by the breeze.
Each step taken with intent,
On this journey, we are bent.

Lessons learned in every turn,
From the flame, our spirits burn.
Purpose guides us like a star,
No matter where we wander far.

Veiled in mystery, the road unfolds,
Stories waiting to be told.
With open hearts, we'll boldly stride,
Through joy, through pain, side by side.

Together, we'll embrace the quest,
Finding solace, seeking rest.
On pathways paved with hope anew,
Our purpose shines, forever true.

The Light of Small Deeds

A gentle smile can change the day,
In small ways, we find our way.
Acts of kindness, simple and bright,
Casting shadows into light.

With each gesture, warmth we share,
Ripples spreading, hearts laid bare.
The smallest deeds, a powerful force,
Guiding souls along their course.

In the quiet moments that we find,
Compassion threads through heart and mind.
A helping hand, a listening ear,
In these moments, love is clear.

So let us shine, both near and far,
Lighting paths like a guiding star.
For in the light of small deeds true,
We find connection, me and you.

Threads of Discipline

In the morning light we weave,
Strength in habits we believe.
Each thread a choice we make,
Building dreams for our own sake.

Patience guides our careful hands,
With focus, we meet our plans.
Step by step, we move ahead,
Through the doubts that fill our head.

As we gather all our might,
Discipline brings forth the light.
In the tapestry of time,
We find purpose in each climb.

With every challenge, we embrace,
The threads of growth we now trace.
Stitching life with heart and will,
In the silence, we find still.

Rising with the Sun

Each dawn, a promise to behold,
A canvas bright, a tale retold.
The sun begins to rise and glow,
In golden hues, the world will grow.

Awake, the birds begin to sing,
Nature's choir, a joyful ring.
With every ray, our spirits soar,
New beginnings at our door.

Embrace the warmth, the light so pure,
In this moment, we find our cure.
With open hearts, we take a chance,
In the sun's glow, we find our dance.

As shadows fade and hope ignites,
The day unfolds with fresh delights.
Rising bold, we stretch and run,
With every heartbeat, rising fun.

Shaping a Brighter Future

In visions clear, we cast our dreams,
Each thought a spark, each choice redeems.
With courage strong and hands that mold,
We shape the path with hearts of gold.

Together, we can break the chain,
Transforming scars into the gain.
We build a world where all belong,
In unity, we find our song.

With every step, we pave the way,
A brighter dawn will greet the day.
With love as our foundation stone,
We rise as one, no longer lone.

As we reach for all that's bright,
We shine our truth, a guiding light.
In every heart, a vision stirs,
Shaping futures that are ours.

The Rhythm of Consistency

In quiet beats, we find our pace,
The steady drum, life's warm embrace.
With every step, we craft our way,
In the rhythm, we choose to stay.

Through highs and lows, we stay in tune,
Chasing dreams beneath the moon.
With focused minds and hearts that yearn,
Each moment brings a chance to learn.

Like waves that crash upon the shore,
Persistence opens every door.
With each repeat, we write our song,
In the rhythm, we all belong.

As we dance through the ebb and flow,
Resilience sets our spirits aglow.
In the pulse of life's sweet song,
The rhythm of consistency keeps us strong.

Breaths Between Each Action

In the silence, a pause unfolds,
Moments linger, stories told.
Each breath whispers, soft and light,
A chance to find what feels just right.

With every step, a thoughtful tread,
Paths diverge, and thoughts are fed.
In the stillness, clarity blooms,
Echoes fade, as kindness looms.

As time drifts through the open air,
Intentions dance, everywhere.
With open hearts, we navigate,
Painting peace, we cultivate.

Together, we weave the unseen thread,
In every word, our spirits spread.
The breaths we take, each action clear,
In mindful moments, we draw near.

A Garden of Gentle Choices

In the garden, seeds are sown,
Each choice brings the light we own.
With tender care, we watch them grow,
Blooms of kindness start to show.

Paths of color, soft and bright,
Dancing under the morning light.
With every thought, a flower might,
Graceful blooms in endless flight.

The whispers of the breeze do share,
In every moment, love and care.
Nurtured gently, each petal gleams,
A tapestry made from our dreams.

Harvesting joy, the heart's sure art,
Gathering wisdom, a brand new start.
We find our place in nature's flow,
In this garden, our spirits glow.

Flux and Flow of Daily Life

Each day unfolds like a dance,
Moments shift, a fleeting chance.
In the rhythm, we find our way,
Navigating the light of day.

With laughter shared, burdens light,
Waves of joy wash over night.
As hours bend but never break,
In the journey, memories make.

The ebb and flow, a tender tide,
Winding paths where dreams reside.
Through challenges, we learn to steer,
In the flow, we shed our fear.

Catch the current, trust the wave,
Breathe in deeply, be a brave.
As life transforms, we will abide,
In flux and flow, we find our pride.

Painting a Brighter Canvas

With every stroke, a story starts,
Colors swirling, dancing hearts.
A canvas wide, with dreams to chase,
In vibrant hues, we find our space.

Brushes dance in hand, so free,
Each color sings a symphony.
In vision clear, we set the tone,
A masterpiece, where love has grown.

Shadows linger, yet bright they gleam,
Painting life like a waking dream.
As we create, our spirits soar,
In every stroke, we find the core.

Together, let our visions blend,
In harmony, we begin to mend.
A brighter picture, bold and true,
With every stroke, we start anew.

Notes from the Path of Progress

With each step forward, we learn,
New heights, new dreams, and hope to burn.
Lessons etched in time's embrace,
Together we rise, we find our place.

Every setback teaches strength,
A winding road, it stretches length.
In the struggle, we find our might,
Guiding us toward the light.

We treasure joy in small things,
The laughter and the love life brings.
Forward onward, we must strive,
In every heartbeat, we revive.

Dreamers gather, hand in hand,
Building futures, a vision grand.
Progress flows like a river wide,
In unity, we take our stride.

Chasing Shadows

In twilight's glow, the shadows dance,
A fleeting glimpse, a wistful chance.
Echoes whisper in the night,
Chasing dreams that take to flight.

Figures loom in soft twilight,
Secrets hidden from our sight.
We pursue a form of grace,
In every shadow, we embrace.

Footfalls soft on silent ground,
Inelusive forms, they gather round.
Through the mist, we start to see,
Chasing shadows that set us free.

Yet in the chase, we find our own,
In darkness, seeds of light are sown.
For what we seek is part of we,
Shadows mold our destiny.

Catching Light

Morning breaks with gentle rays,
Illuminating all our ways.
In stillness, hope and warmth ignite,
Catching dreams in softest light.

Fleeting moments, a whispered thought,
In every glance, a lesson taught.
We reach toward the sky so blue,
With open hearts, we start anew.

Each smile shared is light revealed,
In bonds of love, our fates are sealed.
Through laughter, tears, we pave the way,
Catching light in every day.

As shadows fade and spirits soar,
In every heart, there's so much more.
Together, we will shine so bright,
Chasing dawn, we catch the light.

In Praise of Patience

The river flows, a steady stream,
In patience lies our strongest theme.
Each moment waits, a breath held tight,
In quiet contemplation's light.

Seeds we plant take time to grow,
In silent soil, the roots will show.
With whispered hope, we tend the ground,
In calm resolve, our hearts are found.

Time unwinds in gentle grace,
Through every trial, we find our place.
In each delay, a lesson sways,
In praise of patience, wisdom lays.

For in the waiting, we begin,
To understand the strength within.
With every heartbeat, we embrace,
The beauty found in time and space.

The Power of Now and Here

In the present, life unfolds,
With every breath, a tale retold.
In moments small, we find our peace,
The power of now grants sweet release.

Footsteps quiet on the ground,
In here and now, our hearts are found.
Embracing time with open arms,
We dance to life's most subtle charms.

Worries fade like mist at dawn,
In stillness, we learn to move on.
With gratitude, we start to steer,
The power of now, forever near.

Moments fleeting, yet they remain,
Teaching us in joy and pain.
In every heartbeat, loud and clear,
The magic lies in now and here.

Pulses of Progression

In the heart, a rhythm beats,
Echoes of dreams beneath our feet.
Each step forward, inch by inch,
Confidence grows, fears start to clinch.

The sun rises, a brand new day,
Challenges come, but we find our way.
With every pulse, we learn and grow,
Progress is found in the seeds we sow.

Moments of doubt begin to fade,
Strength emerges, we aren't afraid.
Together we stand, hand in hand,
Pulses of progress across the land.

From whispers of hope, futures arise,
In every setback, a chance to rise.
With hearts ablaze, we chase the light,
Pulses of progress, our guiding sight.

Mosaic of Mindful Moments

Each moment shines, a piece of art,
Colors blend, reflecting the heart.
Fragments of laughter, tears that flow,
In the mosaic, our stories grow.

Breath by breath, we find our grace,
In crowded rooms, or quiet space.
Every glance holds a story shared,
In mindful moments, love is bared.

Nature whispers, in rustling leaves,
The beauty of now, the heart believes.
In tiny pauses, life's truths unfold,
A mosaic of moments, memories gold.

With every sunrise, we start anew,
Grains of sand, the ocean's blue.
In the tapestry of time, we weave,
Mosaic of moments, we dare to believe.

The Dance of Daily Dedication

In shadows cast, we find the light,
With every dawn, our goals in sight.
Step by step, we move with care,
In this dance, we're bold and rare.

Twists and turns, we learn the flow,
With each misstep, our spirits grow.
The rhythm of progress, steady and true,
In dedication, our dreams break through.

Through laughter's joy, and sorrow's tune,
We sway beneath the guiding moon.
With open hearts, we embrace the chance,
In daily dedication, we find our dance.

As seasons change, we hold the beat,
In unity, our lives complete.
With every step, we honor the quest,
The dance of dedication, we give our best.

Shaping Tomorrow's Horizon

With every thought, we plant a seed,
In fertile ground, our visions breed.
Tomorrow's promise, a bright array,
Together we build, come what may.

Hands intertwine, we carve the path,
Turning dreams into a lasting aftermath.
With open minds, we paint the sky,
Shaping horizons, we learn to fly.

In whispered hopes, our futures gleam,
Each shared effort fuels the dream.
As mountains rise, and rivers flow,
Shaping tomorrow, we reap what we sow.

In unity's strength, we find our way,
Crafting a world where dreams can stay.
With hearts aligned, we face the dawn,
Shaping tomorrow, our spirits drawn.

The Awakening of Intent

In the hush of dawn's embrace,
Thoughts bloom like flowers' grace.
Intentions rise with morning light,
Filling hearts with pure delight.

Whispers of purpose softly call,
Guiding us, one and all.
With each step, the path is clear,
Awakening dreams held dear.

In stillness, we find our way,
Nourished by the light of day.
Every choice a sacred dance,
In the rhythm of chance.

Intent, like seeds, we sow,
In the garden of the soul's glow.
As the universe aligns,
Our true essence brightly shines.

Life's Precious Threads

In each moment, a thread weaves tight,
Binding memories, pure and bright.
Through laughter, love, and tears we mend,
Life's precious tapestry, without end.

Colors swirl in vibrant hues,
Stories told in every muse.
Some are frayed, some strong and bold,
Yet each thread is worth its gold.

Connections made across the miles,
With every thread, a myriad of smiles.
Together, we fashion a rich design,
Life's precious threads, eternally intertwine.

So cherish each weave of fate,
For they shape our hearts, innate.
In this fabric, we find our belong,
Life's precious threads, forever strong.

Manifesting Dreams with Action

In the silence of the night, we dream,
Visions shimmering, bright as a beam.
Yet dreams alone do not suffice,
Action ignites the fire's spice.

With courage, we take the first stride,
Breaking boundaries, casting aside.
Each step forward, firm and true,
The world awaits for me and you.

In our hands, the tools of fate,
Crafting greatness, it's never late.
With every choice, we shape the scene,
Manifesting dreams, a vibrant sheen.

The dance of effort and desire,
Fuels the flames, ignites the fire.
Together we rise, we reach the sky,
Manifesting dreams, let them fly.

Days of Our Lives Unfold

Each dawn a canvas, fresh and wide,
In the flow of time, we take our ride.
Moments fade and memories mold,
In the days of our lives, stories told.

With laughter shared and tears that fall,
We're tapestry woven, intricately small.
Through sunlit paths and shadows cast,
The dance of life is rich and vast.

Days blend softly, like a stream,
Chasing shadows of a dream.
In every heartbeat, truth unfolds,
In the days of our lives, joy beholds.

So cherish the journey, embrace the now,
To every moment, take a bow.
For in this tale, we find our role,
In the days of our lives, we become whole.

Morning Light

The sun peeks through the trees,
Whispering warmth to sleepy skies.
Birds begin their morning songs,
As the world starts to arise.

Golden rays touch every leaf,
Casting shadows on the ground.
A canvas painted with soft hues,
In the silence, peace is found.

Coffee brews, the day awakes,
Promises linger in the air.
Each moment a chance to embrace,
The magic that we all can share.

Hope takes flight on gentle beams,
Waking dreams from slumber's hold.
In the morning light, we see,
A day of wonders to unfold.

Evening Reflections

As the sun dips low and sighs,
The sky is painted in deep gold.
Whispers of the day resound,
In shadows soft and tales untold.

The stars peek out, one by one,
A canvas bright against the night.
Memories dance in twilight's glow,
As heart and mind take gentle flight.

In stillness, thoughts begin to weave,
A tapestry of what has been.
Lessons learned and moments shared,
In the quiet, we are seen.

Reflect on dreams that slipped away,
And those that blossomed with the dawn.
In evening's arms, we find our peace,
In the soft embrace of twilight's yawn.

The Dance of Diligence

In quiet corners of the day,
The diligent hearts make their stand.
Steps may falter, but they rise,
With each beat, they understand.

Perseverance leads the way,
With hope as constant guide.
Through the storms of doubt and fear,
They find courage deep inside.

Rhythms of their daily toil,
A melody of grit and grace.
In each task, they find their strength,
In every challenge they embrace.

This dance of diligence endures,
A song that echoes through the years.
In the movement, lives transform,
Through sweat and toil, they shed their fears.

A Tapestry of Persistence

Thread by thread, the weaver works,
Creating patterns rich and bold.
Each struggle a strand interlaced,
In the tapestry, stories told.

Colors blend, and shapes unfold,
A journey marked by highs and lows.
With each knot, resilience grows,
In the fabric, life's essence shows.

Stitches strong, yet delicate,
A testament to what we've faced.
In every twist, a lesson learned,
In every turn, our dreams embraced.

Together woven, hand in hand,
With threads of hope and endless grace.
A tapestry of who we are,
In persistence, we find our place.

The Quiet Strength of Routine

In the rhythm of the day we find,
A comfort in the things we do.
Each moment crafted, deliberate,
In the simple, strength shines through.

Morning rituals set the tone,
Each task a step toward our goal.
Calendar marked with purpose clear,
In routine, we find our role.

As shadows stretch with evening's call,
The gentle patterns reassure.
Through mundanity, we uncover,
A structure that helps us endure.

With quiet strength, we stand our ground,
In the cycles that shape our days.
In the heart of routine's embrace,
We discover life in endless ways.

Seeds of Change in Everyday Soil

In the cracks where shadows play,
Hope is sown beneath the clay.
A tender shoot breaks through the ground,
In quiet strength, new roots are found.

Each small act, a planting hand,
Soft whispers of a vibrant land.
With every drop, the earth absorbs,
Transforming life, as nature scores.

Time flows on, relentless tide,
Yet in stillness, dreams abide.
A garden grows with love and care,
In mundane moments, change is rare.

So let us tend what we can see,
A world reborn, it starts with me.
From everyday, great wonders bloom,
Seeds of change, dispelling gloom.

The Art of Quiet Progress

Slowly moves the river's flow,
In each bend, new tales to grow.
With gentle curves, it finds its way,
A testament to each small day.

The mountain stands, unmoved by time,
Its silent strength, a steady climb.
In stillness lies the deepest heart,
The art of patience plays its part.

Fingers trace the lines of fate,
Each moment holds a choice so great.
With quiet steps, we march along,
In every pause, the soul sings strong.

In shadows cast, we learn to see,
That progress lives in harmony.
The art of quiet, ever bright,
Guides the way from dark to light.

Whispers of Consistency

In the rhythm of the day,
Reliable patterns guide our way.
A heartbeat echoes through the night,
In whispered truths, we find our light.

The dawn arrives with gentle grace,
Repetitive, yet a sacred space.
In every dawn, a promise kept,
A legacy of hope is swept.

Each choice made, a steadfast stone,
Building paths we can call home.
With every brick, foundations rise,
A whispered wish beneath the skies.

So let us weave our stories tight,
In threads of love and pure delight.
Whispers of a life well-lived,
In consistency, the heart is give.

Moments of Grace in the Present

In fleeting glances, time suspends,
Each breath a gift, as meaning blends.
A tender laugh, a gentle touch,
In silent moments, we feel so much.

The sun dips low, embraced by hue,
A canvas painted, old and new.
Stars begin their soft embrace,
In this stillness, find your place.

Through trials faced and joys embraced,
In every moment, love is traced.
Gratitude blooms in hearts so wide,
For the grace that lives inside.

So linger long in present's glow,
Where patience and compassion flow.
Moments of grace, a fleeting art,
In the now, we heal our heart.

The Framework of Focus

In the stillness, thoughts align,
A canvas waiting, pure design.
With purpose clear, we start to build,
A path forward, dreams fulfilled.

Brick by brick, intentions rise,
In focused light, the shadows die.
Each moment captured, a step defined,
In the framework, peace we find.

The choices made, they shape our fate,
In guided thought, we navigate.
As our vision sharpens, doubts will fade,
In the framework, we are laid.

So venture forth with heart in hand,
For focus sows the seeds we've planned.
With clarity, we forge our place,
In the framework, we embrace grace.

Ripple Effects of Kindness

A gentle word, a friendly smile,
Can warm the heart for just a while.
Small acts of care, like drops in streams,
Create the currents of our dreams.

Each gesture shared, a tender thread,
In weaving lives, we're gently led.
The ripples spread, they touch the shore,
Of souls awakened, wanting more.

A helping hand, a listening ear,
Can soothe the pain, dissolve the fear.
With kindness given, we unveil
The strength in love, where hearts prevail.

So let us play our sacred part,
And cast our ripples from the heart.
For in the echoes of what we share,
Kindness blooms everywhere.

The Heartbeat of Habit

In the rhythm of our daily grind,
Habits form, both mild and kind.
With each small choice, we lay the track,
The heartbeat guides us, never slack.

The morning light brings routine near,
A steady pulse, a path so clear.
In actions repeated, we find our flow,
The heartbeat whispers, 'Let's go slow.'

In effort placed, foundations grow,
Through trials faced, we learn to sow.
The heartbeat echoes in what we do,
To shape our lives, we start anew.

So cultivate the habits bright,
That fill the heart with pure delight.
For in the pulse of every day,
The heartbeat leads us on our way.

Curating a Life of Joy

In the gallery of moments caught,
We frame the joy that life has brought.
With colors bright, the laughs we save,
In memories held, the heart's enclave.

Each choice we make, a brushstroke true,
In the canvas wide, of me and you.
With gratitude, we paint our days,
In the light of love, our spirits raise.

So gather beauty, let it shine,
In the simple things, the hearts entwined.
Curate the moments, let them flow,
For in this life, we reap what we sow.

Dance through the chaos, sing through the tears,
For joy endures, beyond our fears.
In the art of living, we find our way,
Curating joy, come what may.

Whispers of Morning Calm

In the early dawn's embrace,
Soft light dances on the lake,
Silence whispers through the trees,
Nature stirs, the day will wake.

Birds begin their gentle song,
Cool breeze brushes past my face,
Each moment feels so right,
In this still, enchanted place.

Misty tendrils weave through air,
Colors bloom in muted grace,
Every breath a soothing balm,
Wrapped in morning's soft embrace.

Hope unfurls like morning dew,
Promises of a brand new start,
With each whisper, peace I find,
Calmness settles in my heart.

Forging Strength in Repetition

In the grind of daily toil,
Each push, a lesson learned,
From struggle, strength shall rise,
In the fire, my spirit burned.

Rhythms pulse within my veins,
Each moment crafted with care,
I build resilience from pain,
Growth is found in repeated dare.

With every fall, a rise anew,
Persistence shapes the soul and mind,
Through the weight, my will will grow,
In the forge, true strength I find.

Cycles weave a sturdy thread,
In the hard work, I am whole,
Forging strength in repetition,
Armor forged around my soul.

Tides of Transformation

Waves roll in, then fade away,
Each crest a new beginning,
Moonlight dances on the sea,
Change is what the tides are bringing.

With each swell, I feel the pull,
A whisper of the world inside,
Letting go, I learn to flow,
Finding strength in every ride.

Seasons shift like ocean's breath,
Currents cradle hopes and dreams,
Transformation's gentle hand,
Crafts our path through life's great streams.

Embrace the flow, let go the shore,
Through the depths, my spirit soars,
Tides of change, forever vast,
In the sea, I find my core.

Harvesting the Present

In the field of now I stand,
Gathering moments like grain,
Each one holds a story tight,
Sweet or bitter, joy or pain.

Beneath the sun's warm embrace,
Life unfolds in vibrant hues,
The present blooms, alive and real,
Each breath a precious muse.

Time slips through like grains of sand,
Yet here in this fleeting bliss,
I find the beauty in the simple,
In every hug and every kiss.

Mindful of each passing hour,
I cherish all that life imparts,
Harvesting the present's gifts,
Sowing love within my heart.

The Lighthouse of Purpose

In storms of doubt, we find our way,
A beacon bright, guiding each day.
With every wave, our hopes arise,
The lighthouse stands, a gift, a prize.

Through fog and fear, we seek the shore,
With every step, we dream for more.
Its light assures, we are not lost,
Embracing love, despite the cost.

Each beam reflects our deepest yearn,
In shadows cast, our spirits burn.
The lighthouse whispers, 'Carry on,'
As night gives way to hopeful dawn.

In pursuit of purpose, hearts unite,
Together we reach toward the light.
For in its glow, we find our peace,
A steadfast guide, our dreams release.

Journeys of the Mind

Wanderlust within my soul,
Thoughts uncharted, dreams unroll.
Each idea a distant star,
In the cosmos, near and far.

Through winding paths, my mind does flow,
In search of truths, it longs to know.
Imaginations take their flight,
Creating worlds, both dark and light.

With every question, mysteries tease,
The universe bends, minds at ease.
Through silent musings, wisdom grows,
In the garden where thought bestows.

Embrace the journey, wild and free,
For in our minds, we learn to be.
With every thought, our spirits soar,
A never-ending quest for more.

Crafting Our Own Path

With trembling hands, we carve our fate,
Each choice we make, we cultivate.
In the forest thick with doubt and fear,
We build our trail, we hold it dear.

Through unmarked roads, our journey leads,
In every step, we plant the seeds.
Resilient hearts, we learn and grow,
Our path unfolds, we start to know.

With open eyes, we seek the light,
The stars above guide through the night.
Each winding turn shapes who we are,
Crafted by dreams that shine like stars.

Together we walk, hand in hand,
Finding strength in the life we've planned.
In crafting paths, we find our way,
Creating futures with each new day.

Moments that Shape Us

In fleeting time, we pause and stare,
Moments whisper secrets laid bare.
Each laugh, each tear, a thread we weave,
In memories' quilt, we dare believe.

Through laughter's echoes, joy ignites,
Within the silence, fear takes flight.
Every heartbeat, a tale to tell,
In moments held, we find our well.

The trials faced, they mold our flesh,
In fire's embrace, we feel refresh.
Each stumble, rise, a lesson learned,
In shadows cast, our spirits burned.

As seasons change, we blossom bold,
In moments shared, our hearts unfold.
Together woven, a tapestry,
In every moment, we find our glee.

Building Bridges of Behavior

In whispers soft, the bridges grow,
Connecting hearts, in ebb and flow.
Through kindness shared, we rise as one,
With every act, a thread begun.

Each simple step, a hand held out,
Dissolving barriers, banishing doubt.
With patience taught and empathy,
We shape a world where all are free.

The laughter shared, a sacred bond,
In unity, we venture fond.
With careful words, we carve the way,
For brighter paths in light of day.

Together we stand, through thick and thin,
With every bridge, a chance to win.
In harmony's embrace, we dwell,
Building dreams, where love can swell.

The Rhythm of Simple Acts

In every gesture, a silent beat,
Lives intertwined, in joy and heat.
A smile exchanged, the world ignites,
Simple acts, turning days to nights.

A helping hand in times of need,
The smallest deed can plant the seed.
In each heartbeat, a rhythm flows,
With kindness rich, the spirit grows.

A door held wide, a heart laid bare,
In the echo of care, we find our share.
Every moment, a chance to give,
Through simple acts, we truly live.

The dance of life, with love as key,
In every action, we are free.
Embrace the rhythm, let it sing,
For in simplicity, joy takes wing.

Flickers of Intent in Motion

In quiet moments, sparks ignite,
Intentions pure, set forth in light.
A glance exchanged, a breath held tight,
Flickering hopes, taking flight.

With every choice, we weave a tale,
Through winding paths, we shall not fail.
Each step we take, a vision clear,
In motion's grace, we persevere.

The heart's deep whisper guides the hand,
As flickers glow, we understand.
In unity, we brave the storm,
With courage found, our spirits warm.

Through flickers bright, intentions bloom,
Transforming darkness into room.
The dance, the flow, the beating heart,
In every moment, we play our part.

Dawn of Gentle Transformations

As dawn breaks soft, a world anew,
Gentle transformations come to view.
With every ray, a chance to grow,
In humble hearts, the seeds we sow.

Through trials faced, we learn and bend,
A tapestry of strength we send.
With gentle hands, we mold the clay,
Transforming night into the day.

The whispers of change, a tender song,
In every heart, we all belong.
As shadows fade and colors soar,
We welcome light, forevermore.

In unity, we navigate the tides,
In gentle ways, the truth abides.
A dawn of hope, through love's embrace,
Transforms our world, a sacred space.

Tuning into Tomorrow

In whispers of dawn, hopes ignite,
Dreams take flight on the edge of night.
With every breath, futures unfold,
A symphony waits in the warmth and cold.

Eyes to the horizon, we venture forth,
Guided by stars in the vast, dark north.
Every heartbeat syncs to the time,
Resonating softly, a rhythmic rhyme.

The pulse of the earth, beneath our feet,
Speaks of journeys, adventures to greet.
In the stillness, we glean the sign,
Tuning our minds as the stars align.

So let us embrace, with courage complete,
The song of tomorrow, where dreams compete.
With open hearts, we shall ignite,
The promise of dawn, glowing bright.

The Serenity of Structure

In gardens of order, calm resides,
Where chaos with beauty neatly divides.
Lines of design in nature's embrace,
Crafting a world where peace finds its place.

Sturdy branches rise, roots run deep,
Holding the earth in a tender keep.
Each leaf a story, each stone a friend,
In the symphony where elements blend.

Embracing the rhythm, the pulse of the land,
A sanctuary built by nature's hand.
In every corner, serenity thrums,
Echoing softly, a whisper of drums.

We journey through pathways of measured grace,
Finding each structure a warm, sweet embrace.
With peace in our hearts, we create what will,
A tapestry woven with time, breath, and skill.

Adventures on the Familiar Path

Beneath the boughs of an ancient tree,
Lie stories etched in the air, carefree.
Each step along this well-worn way,
Leads to the heart of another day.

Familiar sights, yet new eyes see,
Unexpected wonders that set minds free.
The rustle of leaves, the call of a bird,
Speak a language that's often unheard.

With every turn, the path welcomes change,
Unraveling mysteries, both bold and strange.
Roots intertwine like tales we've spun,
Each moment a gift, every stride, a run.

Together we wander, together we roam,
Finding adventure where we call home.
In the heart of the mundane, we find our spark,
In the glow of twilight, we light the dark.

The Power of Steady Steps

Each step we take is a promise made,
In the quiet, the noise begins to fade.
With purpose as guide, we choose our pace,
Courage emerges, a warm embrace.

Through valleys of doubt, to mountains of hope,
With the strength within, we learn to cope.
Balance and rhythm in every stride,
Trusting the journey, our hearts open wide.

In moments of struggle, we find our ground,
The power of movement, profound and sound.
One foot in front, as the path unfolds,
Stories of triumph, the future beholds.

Together we march, through storms and sun,
In unity, knowing we are not done.
With every heartbeat, we've come so far,
The power of steady steps guides us—our star.

Pearls of Patience

In silence deep, the moments grow,
Each breath a whisper, seeds we sow.
Time stretches soft like gentle clay,
We shape our dreams in a patient way.

With every trial, we learn to bend,
Strength in waiting, a kind of mend.
The storm will pass, the sun will shine,
In pearls of patience, our hopes align.

Each heartbeat counts, a step to take,
In the quiet dawn, we waken fate.
Embracing stillness, finding light,
The journey unfolds in the softest night.

Through winding paths, we find our way,
Crafting peace from the fray of day.
In the tapestry of time, we weave,
The art of waiting, we dare believe.

The Canvas of Continuous Growth

Brush strokes of time, colors blend,
On the canvas, visions transcend.
Each layer built, a life anew,
In every shade, potential shines through.

Seeds planted deep in fertile ground,
Roots intertwine, where dreams abound.
With patience and care, we cultivate,
The art of growth, we celebrate.

Seasons will change, but we stay true,
The canvas expands, there's more to view.
Each challenge faced, a stroke of grace,
In the masterpiece, we find our place.

Brush in hand, we paint our fate,
The journey is bold, never late.
With open hearts and minds that soar,
Continuous growth, forever explore.

Nurturing the Seeds of Change

In hands of hope, we hold the dreams,
Nurtured gently, or so it seems.
Watered with care, we watch them sprout,
These seeds of change, what life's about.

With every heartbeat, courage grows,
In the soil rich, the future flows.
Through storms and sun, we tend with grace,
Each step forward, a new embrace.

The winds may shift, and paths may bend,
Yet in our hearts, we find the blend.
With patience vast, and love as guide,
Nurturing dreams, with arms open wide.

As seasons pass, we bloom and thrive,
In the garden of life, we come alive.
The seeds of change in us reside,
A tapestry where hope will abide.

A Symphony of Morning Routines

Morning light creeps through the haze,
A symphony starts, setting the phase.
Birds take flight, they greet the dawn,
In tranquil moments, the day is drawn.

With gentle stretches, we find our breath,
In each movement, there's life, not death.
Coffee brews with a fragrant sigh,
Awakening senses, we rise and fly.

Pages turn in a book of dreams,
Each routine flows like gentle streams.
With gratitude, we find our way,
In a symphony crafted for the day.

As moments linger, together we flow,
In morning's embrace, our spirits grow.
A dance of rituals sets the tone,
In this sweet symphony, we find our home.

Gentle Waves of Change

The tide rolls in, soft and slow,
Whispers of dreams in the undertow.
Every crest brings a chance to be,
A wave of hope, wild and free.

Moments shift like grains of sand,
Shaping lives as we take a stand.
Flowing forward, we ride the swell,
In changing tides, our stories dwell.

With every ebb, a lesson learned,
In quiet depths, our passions burned.
Embrace the current's gentle pull,
For in the change, our hearts are full.

So let us dance on the ocean's face,
Unite with courage, find our place.
In gentle waves, we find our way,
Transforming dusk into the day.

A Celebration of Small Victories

In the morning light, we rise anew,
With every breath, a journey in view.
Little wins, like stars that shine,
Illuminate paths, so divine.

A smile shared, a door held wide,
A helping hand by our side.
In humble acts, great strength we find,
In small victories, love intertwined.

Each step forward, a story told,
Moments precious, a treasure to hold.
Celebrate each laugh, each tear,
For in these moments, we persevere.

Together we'll cherish the little things,
In harmony, that joy brings.
With gratitude, our hearts ignite,
A celebration, pure and bright.

The Promise of Everyday

In the dawn's embrace, the world awakes,
A canvas fresh, each choice it makes.
Promises linger in the morning air,
Hope is woven everywhere.

With every sunrise, a chance anew,
To chase our dreams, to break on through.
Embrace the mundane, find beauty there,
In simple moments, love's sweet care.

The quiet whispers, secrets untold,
In laughter, warmth, and hands to hold.
Amidst the rush, let us find grace,
In the promise shared, a sacred space.

Through trials faced, together we'll stand,
In everyday miracles, hand in hand.
For life's true treasure, bold and bright,
Is the promise of love, day and night.

Foundations Beneath Our Feet

Roots run deep in the earth below,
Holding us steady as we grow.
Invisible threads that bind us tight,
Foundations strong, in shadows and light.

Through storms and trials, we'll remain,
Supported by love, through joy, through pain.
Every crack and fissure tells a tale,
Of courage found when we prevail.

In whispered wisdom, ancient and true,
We build our lives, made fresh and new.
With every step, we recognize,
The strength within, the will to rise.

Together we stand on this sacred ground,
In unity, our voices resound.
For every heartbeats, a promise we keep,
Foundations beneath, our dreams run deep.

Weaving Threads of Intent

In quiet moments, threads are spun,
Each thought a color, bright as the sun.
With careful hands, we weave our dreams,
A tapestry formed from whispered themes.

Intentions clear as a morning dew,
With every stitch, our essence comes true.
Patterns emerge, both complex and fine,
A fabric of hopes, intertwined in time.

Consistency in the Canvas

With steady strokes, the lines are drawn,
Each hue a promise, from dusk till dawn.
A canvas waits for the artist's hand,
To manifest visions, bright and grand.

In every detail, persistence persists,
Crafting a picture that gently insists.
Through trials faced, the colors blend,
Creating stories that never end.

A Garden of Intentions

In fertile soil, ideas take root,
Nurtured by dreams, they blossom and shoot.
Each seed of hope, a wish to fulfill,
In the garden of life, we tend with will.

Sunshine and rain both play their part,
Cultivating growth, awakening art.
Petals unfurl, revealing their grace,
In this lush haven, we find our place.

The Alchemy of Daily Choices

Each day unfolds, a chance to create,
Turning the mundane to something great.
With choices made, our path is laid,
In the alchemy of life, we're unafraid.

Moments collide, a spark ignites,
Transforming shadows into bright lights.
With courage found in the tiniest act,
We mold our fate, both swift and exact.

Painting Dreamscapes with Discipline

In quiet hours, colors blend,
Each stroke a thought, each hue a friend.
Patience weaves through every line,
Crafting visions, pure and fine.

With steady hands, the canvas waits,
Dreams emerge from mindful states.
A dance of light, a play of shade,
In every detail, brilliance laid.

Focus sharpens, a guiding force,
Through chaos, we find our course.
Layers build, both soft and bold,
A story in pigments, gently told.

In the end, what dreams unite,
Is discipline wrapped in pure delight.
Each masterpiece a journey vast,
Where heart and craft forever last.

Wisps of Inspiration in Action

Thoughts like fireflies flicker bright,
Dancing softly in the night.
Chasing shadows, grasping light,
Inspiration takes its flight.

Whispers float on gentle breeze,
Carrying tales that aim to please.
Ideas bloom like springtime flowers,
In the stillness, hidden powers.

Every moment is a spark,
Lighting up the deepest dark.
With each breath, creation stirs,
In the silence, music purrs.

From wisps to forms, a vibrant change,
Through action, nothing feels strange.
Inspiration fuels the fire,
To bring forth what we truly desire.

The Architecture of Tomorrow

Skyscrapers reach for the sky,
Bold structures where dreams comply.
Each angle counts, each line precise,
A vision born, a sacrifice.

Foundations laid with hopes of change,
In every brick, a world rearranged.
Sculpted spaces, both wide and close,
Whispers of life, diverse and engrossed.

Nature blends with steel and glass,
A harmony that dares to pass.
Parks and pathways intertwine,
In the future, a grand design.

From blueprints deep, to soaring heights,
We craft a dance of days and nights.
The architecture of tomorrow sings,
With every heartbeat, possibility brings.

Simple Acts, Lasting Impact

A smile shared, a hand to lend,
In these moments, hearts we mend.
Small gestures whisper kindness true,
A ripple in the world that grew.

In quiet spaces, love can thrive,
Simple acts keep hope alive.
Each word a balm, each touch a guide,
In every avenue, compassion rides.

From seeds we plant, the harvest's wide,
Together strong, we stand with pride.
With every choice, the chance to shift,
To create change is the greatest gift.

In the end, it's clear we find,
The impact lies in hearts combined.
For in the details, love reacts,
Changing lives with simple acts.

Threads of Routine Woven Softly

In early light, the day unfolds,
With gentle steps, a story told.
Each moment stitched with care and grace,
A pattern formed in time and space.

Sipping tea, a quiet pause,
In every breath, a silent cause.
Weaving joy in daily chore,
Threads of life, forevermore.

Within the rhythm, comfort lies,
A tapestry beneath the skies.
With every sun that rises high,
Routine and love, we can't deny.

The Symphony of Steady Choices

In every moment, a note to play,
A harmony that leads the way.
With steady hands, we craft our tune,
A dance of life beneath the moon.

The choices made, like beats that flow,
Together shaping what we sow.
In vibrant colors, each step sings,
A symphony of simple things.

Resonant sounds of love and care,
A melody that fills the air.
Together in this timeless space,
Steady choices leave their trace.

Tiny Triumphs at Dawn

In the hush before the sun,
A whisper of success begun.
With every dawn, new chances rise,
Tiny triumphs in the skies.

A stretch, a yawn, the day awakes,
In small steps, the heart partakes.
Each little win, a spark of light,
Guiding us through day and night.

Moments cherished, so profound,
With open eyes, the world is found.
Tiny triumphs, brave and true,
In every heart, they shine anew.

Echoes of Mindful Living

With every breath, a chance to see,
The beauty held in what can be.
In mindful steps, we find our way,
Echoes linger, bright and gay.

In silence, wisdom softly speaks,
In gratitude, our spirit peaks.
Each moment cherished, each thought clear,
Echoes of love that draw us near.

Together in this gentle space,
We find our truth, we find our grace.
In mindful living, life takes flight,
Echoes remain, hearts burning bright.

Building Bridges with Routine

In morning light, our paths align,
We start anew, with dreams that shine.
Each simple task, a step we take,
Building bridges, not to break.

The coffee brews, a warm embrace,
Familiar smiles, a friendly space.
Through daily rhythms, bonds grow strong,
Together we sing our shared song.

In twilight's glow, we pause to see,
How routines weave our tapestry.
With every heartbeat, trust is found,
In quiet moments, love is bound.

And as the stars begin to gleam,
We find our hopes within a dream.
In routine's arms, we find our way,
Building bridges, come what may.

The Compass of Commitment

With every promise, a path we chart,
A compass guides the hopeful heart.
Through storms and calm, we stand as one,
With steadfast love, our journey's begun.

Adventurous goals, we hold so dear,
In every challenge, we persevere.
Through ups and downs, we learn and grow,
The compass points where love will flow.

In laughter shared and whispered dreams,
Our bond grows deeper than it seems.
With every step, we dare to take,
The compass of commitment makes.

With unwavering faith, we face the night,
Together, we embrace the light.
Through thick and thin, we'll find our way,
The compass guides us, come what may.

Rewiring Our Days

In morning hush, we find our core,
A chance to change, to soar once more.
Each moment lived, a thread to weave,
Rewiring days, a new reprieve.

With open minds, we seek to learn,
In every action, watch the fire burn.
Old habits fade as fresh ones rise,
Rewiring paths under open skies.

In stillness found, we gather strength,
To stretch our limits, grow in length.
With courage bold, we take a stand,
Rewiring life, hand in hand.

At dusk we pause, reflect a while,
In every challenge, we find our style.
Each day anew, we forge our fate,
Rewiring days, it's never too late.

Moments of Clarity

In the rush of life, we pause to find,
Moments of clarity, peace of mind.
Through swirling thoughts, a gentle breeze,
We find our truth, our hearts at ease.

The clock ticks slow in a whispered hour,
Each second blooms like a vibrant flower.
In these rare times, wisdom flows,
Moments of clarity, beauty grows.

With open hearts, we see the light,
Guided by stars that shine so bright.
In silence shared, we understand,
Moments of clarity, hand in hand.

As shadows fade and dawn awakes,
We treasure each moment that life makes.
In clarity found, we choose to see,
These moments shape our destiny.

9 789916 882801